Introduct

Stretching **north** from the Wye Vall
Hay-on-Wye, lies a wealth of open a
river valleys. Four 'A' roads enclose
land, which is bisected by the 'B' road runn...
Valley to a point a few miles to the west of Kington in Herefordshire. The
'B' road also serves as something of a boundary, between the open access
land to the north and west and the mainly lower-lying farmland, woodland
and villages to the south and east.

The River Arrow has its source in this area, before flowing east to
Kington and on into England. A few miles further to the west, the Edw
follows its course to the junction with the Wye. There are numerous smaller
watercourses in the area, as well as two lakes and a considerable number of
hill top ponds.

This is an area rich in history, with prehistoric remains including hill
forts, stone circles and house platforms. There is also plentiful evidence of
Norman occupation, with castle sites at Painscastle, Hundred House and
Gwaunceste Hill. You will also find a variety of old churches, many in the
circular churchyards that indicate the location of a pre-Christian sacred
site. Wells were also plentiful in the area, including the site of a sacred well
and one now within a public house.

During the later nineteenth century Francis Kilvert, the Victorian cleric
and diarist, walked extensively in this area while curate at Clyro recording
his impressions of the countryside and its occupants. Some of the country
houses he visited can be seen during the walks.

Although lacking in present day public transport, this is an area with
a wide variety of accommodation from hotels to camping sites, including
a number of public houses. Regular bus services do run along the Wye
Valley to the south and the A44 to the north. Details of the services can be
obtained from Powys County Council on 0845 607 6060 or www.powysbus.
info

The use of walking boots and suitable clothing for walks in this guide
is recommended. Walkers are also advised to check weather forecasts,
particularly if following upland paths (phone no 09068 505 315 for details).
The location of each walk is shown on the outside back cover, and their
starting points and features are summarised inside the back cover, together
with estimated walking times. Allow extra time if you are exploring places
of interest on or near the route.

Please follow the country code – *and enjoy your walking!*

WALK I
NEW & OLD RADNOR

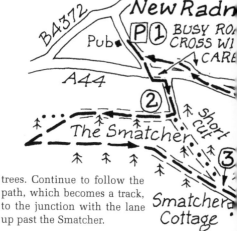

DESCRIPTION A moderate walk, with one fairly steep climb in the first section. This 8¼ mile route includes mixed and deciduous woodland, field paths and lanes, with a variety of good views over the Radnor Valley. The mid-point of the walk, at Old Radnor, is adjacent to St Stephen's Church, where there are information boards on the history of the Radnor Valley, together with a plaque identifying the various hills visible across the valley. The Harp Inn is close by (*limited opening*). NB Some of the fields crossed in the neighbourhood of Stone's Farm and while en route from there to the lane near Harpton Farm are used for cereal crops – *please take care to avoid damage to these.* Allow about 5 hours for the walk.

PUBLIC TRANSPORT Powys Bus 39 (Llandrindod Wells to Kington, for Hereford), stops in New Radnor.

START Roadside parking in New Radnor, SO 214607.

1 From the street near the Radnor Arms, head past the Cornewall Lewis Memorial to the junction with the main road. Cross the main road with care and head LEFT for a short distance to a lane leading off to the right. Follow this uphill for a short way and then turn RIGHT on a track leading into The Smatcher. (NB it is possible to shorten this part of the walk by continuing up the lane and rejoining the main route at instruction **3** – this involves a shorter but steeper climb).

2 Follow the main track through the wood until reaching a place where the track broadens out and begins to descend slightly. At this point, head HALF LEFT on a path that climbs the hill. Keep a look out for a wooden fence ahead – on sighting this, look out for a narrow path leading sharp left from the main path. Turn onto this path, which soon broadens out, and follow it along the hill and back into woodland, where it follows an established path past two or three fallen trees. Continue to follow the path, which becomes a track, to the junction with the lane up past the Smatcher.

3 Turn RIGHT and follow the lane past Smatcher Cottage to a T junction. Head slightly to the RIGHT and start down an enclosed track. Follow this downhill and then on a slight rise to a further road junction. Turn RIGHT and almost immediately turn LEFT, passing to the left of the former chapel at Yardro.

4 Take the left fork at the next junction. Follow the lane for some way, passing the houses called The Row. From this point, look out for a footpath sign on the left, just before reaching further houses. Turn LEFT onto this path, go through a waymarked gate and past a waymark sign on an old gatepost. Follow the left hand side of the field to a waymarked gate. Continue along the left hand side of the next field to the far corner.

5 Do not cross the old stile here, but remain in the field, turning RIGHT and continuing to follow the left hand boundary of the field. Go through a gate and continue along the left hand side of the next field to reach a gate onto a track. The official route of the footpath, which goes behind the house at Stone's Farm, is currently hard to find from this end – the current owner has suggested following the track past the house at this point and continuing along the lane into Old Radnor.

6 On reaching a junction, cross and go into St Stephen's churchyard. When ready, exit on the far side where the Harp Inn will be seen on the other side of a parking area. *There are also two benches adjacent to the churchyard, with information boards and a landscape plaque just beyond these.*

across the next field to reach a waymarked footbridge. Head HALF LEFT across a further field to reach a gate just to the left of the wood. Continue along the left hand side of the field to two waymarked gates at the far end (passing a waymark sign on route). Follow the right hand side of the final field to a stile onto a lane.

9 Turn LEFT and follow the lane for a short distance to a waymark post and steps leading up to a gate on the right. Follow this footpath into and through Frostal Wood, eventually coming to a further waymarked gate on the far side. Pass under an old railway bridge and turn RIGHT (*The definitive course of the footpath [leading to the left] has become overgrown. In practice, most walkers turn right and follow the course of the old railway line. A Powys County Council Rights of Way Officer has discussed the matter with the landowner and advises that the old railway line route should be used, unless waymarking subsequently indicates otherwise*). Join a track and turn LEFT, following the track to the junction with the main road.

7 When ready, go back past the church and retrace the outward route until reaching the first of the barns at Stone's Farm. Turn RIGHT and go through a gate immediately before the first barn. Head down the field, keeping to the right of the row of trees. Look for and follow a short track down to a waymarked gate into Stone's Coppice. Follow the course of an old track through the wood to a further waymarked gate.

8 Follow the left hand side of the next field and go through an old gateway on the left. Head HALF RIGHT across the next field to a waymarked gate tucked away just to the left of the trees. Bear HALF LEFT

10 Turn LEFT and follow the verge of the main road, with care, until reaching the entrance to a lay-by on the left (the course of the old road). Follow this until the junction with the new main road. Continue along the main road for a short distance until reaching a no-through lane on the right. Go along the no-through lane and continue along the path at the end, to reach the road leading into New Radnor.

3

WALK 2
SMATCHER & BURL

DESCRIPTION An energetic 8¾ mile walk heading south from New Radnor and then following bridleways westwards along the ridge, with views across the valley to Radnor Forest. Looping round to the south, the route then crosses the open access land on Burl Hill, before following a mixture of lane, footpath, track and bridleway to rejoin the outward route to New Radnor via the Smatcher. Allow about 5¼ hours for the walk.

PUBLIC TRANSPORT Powys Bus 39 (Llandrindod Wells to Kington, for Hereford), stops in New Radnor.

START Roadside parking/bus stop in New Radnor, SO 214607.

I From the roadside parking/bus stop, head towards the eastern exit from the village to the A44. Cross the main road with care and head LEFT along the verge for a short way, to a turning on the right. Go along this lane, passing the entrance to Old Station Caravan Park (on the left). Follow the lane uphill, steeply for a time. Pass Smatcher Cottage, on the right, and continue to a road junction. Turn RIGHT. On reaching the entrance to Stockenny Farm, take the right hand, waymarked, gate.

2 Follow the track along the left hand side of the field. Take the right fork in the track, continuing to follow the left hand side of the field. Go through a gate into a plantation and continue AHEAD on the main track, ignoring a side track leading in from the right. Towards the far side of the plantation, follow the track round to the left and through a gate.

3 Immediately turn RIGHT and go through a second waymarked gate. Head along the left hand side of the field to a further waymarked gate. Continue STRAIGHT AHEAD across the field to reach a track that leads between a tree (on the left) and fence (on the right). Follow the track to the left of the fence. Pass through two waymarked gates. Head HALF RIGHT on a descending track. When the track turns sharp right, continue AHEAD to a waymarked gate.

4 Pass through the gate and head along the right hand side of the field. On reaching a waymarked junction of tracks, bear LEFT. Continue to follow the right hand boundary of the field, passing two waymark signs on fenceposts. Pass through a waymarked gate and continue along the right hand side of the next field. Join a farm track by a waymark post on the left. Bear RIGHT on the farm track. Pass a waymark post on the right and keep to the left of the fence, following the base of the hill. Towards the end of the field, climb HALF LEFT to a waymarked gate.

5 Follow the track along the right hand side of the field, descending and then ascending once more, to reach a gate near a four-way way-mark post. Go through

the gate and follow the track ahead, along the left hand side of the field. Go through the waymarked gate at the end and turn LEFT. Follow the left hand side of the field for a few yards to a further waymarked gate. Follow the track along the next two fields, connected by a gate. Pass a waymark post on the right and follow the track between fences. Pass through two gates, the first waymarked.

4

6 Follow the track past a group of trees on the left. Pass through a way-marked gate and take the right fork (the 'red arrow' route). Pass through a further gate, with a pond on the right just beyond this. The stony track ahead is the most direct route across Burl Hill. Since this is open access land, walkers with maps/navigational skills may prefer to divert to the

right, head uphill and then to the left on some of the network of tracks and paths used by horseriders, to reach the highest point of Burl Hill, towards the eastern end. This is certainly well worth it for the 360 degree views.

Having done so, return to the stony track by heading left down a grassy track to the north easterly corner of the hill. Follow the stony track to the junction with a tarmac lane.

7 Follow the lane to the point where this bends to the right, near a shed on the left. Cross a waymarked stile to the right of the shed and head along the right hand side of the field to the next stile. Continue along the right hand side of the next field, until reaching a stile on the right just beyond a

gate. Cross and head LEFT along the track. Pass the first gate on the right (currently fallen). At the point where the track makes a sharp bend to the left, cross a small area of damp ground to reach a gate on the right.

8 Follow the right hand side of the field. Towards the far side, bear SLIGHTLY TO THE LEFT to reach a stile. Cross and head HALF RIGHT down the bank through the trees to reach a footbridge and stile. Bear HALF RIGHT and follow the right hand side of the field to reach a stile into a wood. Follow the path through the wood to reach an unsurfaced highway track. Turn LEFT on this and follow it, ignoring a footpath sign leading to the right. Pass through a gate and join a lane.

9 Turn LEFT on the lane. After a few yards, go through an unmarked gate on the right, with a track beyond. Head DIAGONALLY across the field to a gate in the far corner. Follow the track along the left hand side of the next field. Pass through a gate and continue to follow the track on an uphill course across the middle of a further field. Pass through a gate and continue part way along the right hand side of the next field, then go through a gate on the right. Head along the left hand side of the field, pass through a further gate and follow the right hand side of the field to a waymarked junction of bridleways.

10 Turn RIGHT and go through the gate into a plantation. Follow the path AHEAD and then round to the right. Continue AHEAD to the gate at the far end of the plantation. Continue AHEAD along the right hand side of the field, being joined by another track coming from the right. Follow the track through a gate onto a lane near the entrance to Stockenny Farm. Continue AHEAD to the junction and turn LEFT, following the lane past Smatcher Cottage and back down past the Smatcher to the junction with the main road. Cross with care and head LEFT along the verge to the turning for New Radnor.

Map labels: P 1 New Radnor; A44; CROSS WITH CARE!; walk 1; walk 1; Smatcher Cottage; 2; Stockenny Farm; walk 1; 3; 10; 9; F.B.; 8; 7

LLYNHEILYN, BLACK YAT & GWAUNCESTE HILL

DESCRIPTION An energetic walk of some 8 miles, following an attractive lane along a valley before joining a track across fields, passing an upland lake and the remains of an old cottage at Black Yatt, to reach open access land. A meandering climb to the trig point on Gwaunceste Hill is followed by the use of bridleways with a range of views, passing a possible castle site, to rejoin the road near a lake glimpsed on the outward journey. The ascent of Gwaunceste Hill follows a route used by horseriders and others but it is not indicated on the current OS Explorer map – although details of visual reference points are included, navigational skills and aids are highly recommended for use with this route. Allow about 4¾ hours for the walk.

START Roadside lay-by on A44 just north west of Fforest Inn junction, SO 171585.

PUBLIC TRANSPORT Powys Bus 46 (Llandrindod Wells to Hereford) via the A44.

1 From roadside parking, follow the A44 south to the junction with the A481, by the Forest Inn public house. Turn RIGHT and follow the A481 for about ¼ mile. Turn LEFT into a no-through lane. Follow this to the end, by Foice Farm Boarding Kennels.

2 On reaching the end of the lane, continue AHEAD through the waymarked gate. Follow the track along the left hand side of the field. Pass the site of a small disused quarry and follow the track on a gradual ascent to the next waymarked gate. Continue to follow the track along the left hand side of the field, to reach a waymark post on the left, near a gate.

3 Do not go through the gate but turn RIGHT here, passing to the right hand side of a small pond. Head HALF RIGHT up the field to reach a gate in the far right corner. Go through the gate and follow the track along the left hand side of the field. Pass a waymark post on the right, by sheep pens. Pass to the left of Llanwentre Pool and join a stony track that veers towards the left.

4 Follow the stony and then grassy track, passing through a waymarked gate. Continue to follow the track as this bears generally towards the right across the next long field. Go through another waymarked gate and follow the stony track ahead, soon coming to the ruins of the dwelling at Black Yatt ('*Up the Claerwen' by Sid Wright, 1948, refers to Black Yatt as a pre-World War II shepherd's dwelling*). Continue to follow the track, passing to the left of an area of conifers and crossing a shallow ford. At a junction of waymarked tracks, continue AHEAD (on the 'red arrow' route) to reach a gate onto the open access land at Gwaunceste Hill.

5 Follow the track AHEAD along the open access area until reaching a junction with three other tracks, one leading up Cnwch Bank on the left. Turn SHARP RIGHT on a stony track that soon becomes grassy surfaced. Follow this winding track uphill. When the gradient eases cross two small streams and soon bear RIGHT on a faint track leading uphill. Cross a grassy area, after which the course of the track becomes clearer. Continue along the track (which can be faint in places) using the valley off to the left as a visual reference point.

6 Follow the track as it gradually bears half left and crosses further damp ground. Follow the track half right, above a large, treelined dingle on the left. (At this point there is a sighting of two trees on the skyline, which are quite close to the Gwaunceste Hill trig point). Follow the track as it veers half right and then turns left, head-

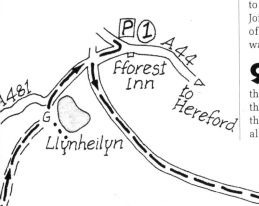

to reach a tall waymark post on a slight rise. Join a grassy track that passes just to the left of the waymark post and follow this to a waymarked gate.

9 Pass through the gate and head along the left hand side of the field, on a route that quite soon becomes a grassy track. Pass through another waymarked gate and follow the right hand side of the next field, eventually descending towards Llynheilyn. Turn

ing towards the two trees. Cross a further small stream and continue along the track, which passes to the left of the trees and then veers right. Follow the track towards the trig point that is now visible ahead – the easiest way to reach this is by striking off from the track on sheep paths.

7 When ready, retrace the outward route from the trig point for a short way, using a path that connects at right angles with another path. Turn RIGHT and follow the second path downhill until reaching a field boundary on the right. Turn RIGHT and follow the wide track along the edge of the open access land. Ignore a bridleway sign on the left. Pass to the right of a circular pond with an island in the middle. Keep to the main track, as this crosses through heather moorland – *the views include Llandegley Rocks* – and then descends. Cross rocky areas of track and soon after bear HALF RIGHT to a waymarked gate.

8 Follow the grassy track AHEAD, passing to the left of another pond, to reach a 3-way marker post. (*The line of four/five stones leading to a mound marks the remains of the possible motte and bailey castle*). Continue STRAIGHT AHEAD across the open ground

RIGHT through a waymarked gate and very soon turn LEFT. Follow the track for a few yards to the junction with the A481. Turn RIGHT and follow the main road to the junction by the Fforest Inn.

WALK 4
HERGEST RIDGE

DESCRIPTION A 3¾ mile moderate route with a climb at the start up to and around the western, Welsh, part of Hergest ridge. The route includes an excellent view down onto Gladestry village and towards the hills beyond as well as extensive views north to Radnor Forest and south towards the Black Mountains. Pub in village with limited opening hours (01544 370669). Allow about 2¼ hours for the walk.
START Roadside parking in Gladestry village, SO 233552.

I From the roadside parking, take the Huntington road out of Gladestry. After a couple of hundred yards, take the no-through lane leading up to the left (signed for Offa's Dyke Path). Follow the lane up through two gates and onto open access land. Continue to follow the track ahead and then round to the left until reaching Offa's Dyke Path waymark posts on both sides of the track.

2 Turn LEFT here, leaving Offa's Dyke Path, and follow the wide grassy track uphill and towards the western end of Hergest Ridge for a view down onto Gladestry and the hills beyond. When ready retrace the outward route back to the paired waymark posts. Continue along Offa's Dyke Path for a short way until reaching a junction of tracks near the next waymark post.

3 Leave Offa's Dyke Path here and take the wide grassy track on the left. Follow this up and across the brow of the hill. Take the left fork at a junction of tracks and continue AHEAD until rejoining the course of Offa's Dyke Path (near a waymark post on the right shortly before reaching a bracken-free area).

4 Turn SHARP RIGHT onto Offa's Dyke Path and follow this back towards Gladestry. Pass a single waymark post and continue along the track, passing to the right of a small hill. At the paired waymark posts, follow the track round to the left and descend back down through the two gates to the Huntington road. Turn RIGHT towards Gladestry, turning LEFT at the next junction to return to the roadside parking area.

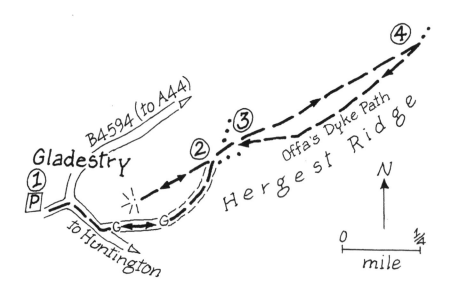

WALK 5

GLASCWM HILL

DESCRIPTION An energetic climb by road is followed by a more gradual bridleway ascent onto Glascwm Hill. The walk then heads along the ridge, providing a range of excellent views (Black Mountains and Brecon Beacons included). The final stages of the walk descend towards Glascwm, rejoining the road near the village church. The total walk is 4 miles long. Allow about 2½ hours for the walk.

START Glascwm Village, SO 158533.

1 From the area of the green, follow the road up Rhiw Fwnws, crossing a cattle grid. On reaching police notices at the brow of the hill (No motor vehicles on open land except for local access) turn RIGHT and follow the track running to the left of the enclosed fields.

2 At the end of the fields, remain with the track as this heads slightly to the right. At the fork in the track, bear LEFT. Continue to follow the grassy track uphill and through two bends to the left.

3 At a junction of tracks, turn SHARP RIGHT on a wide track that now follows the ridgeline along Glascwm Hill. In due course, pass a small boundary stone on the left. Cross a small summit and pass a hill pool on the right. At the junction with a track coming from the right, bear LEFT.

4 Descend for a few yards then, when the main track bears left, turn RIGHT on a side track. On reaching a further junction of tracks, near a wooden post off to the left, turn RIGHT again. Follow the track, which becomes a stony path, over the brow of the hill and over the shoulder of the next hill.

5 At a junction of paths, head RIGHT. Follow the path, which soon becomes a grassy track that steadily descends. Go RIGHT at a junction near trees. After a few feet, bear LEFT on a path that descends just to the right of the trees. Go through a gate and down a short track to a road. Turn RIGHT and follow the road back to Glascwm.

WALK 6
ABEREDW HILL

DESCRIPTION There is an energetic climb at the start of this 7¼ mile walk, from the roadside parking area to the top of the open access hill. This is certainly well worth the ascent for the range of excellent views over the Wye and other valleys to the hill ranges beyond. Aberedw Hill is the site of numerous hilltop ponds and small lakes, as well as several tumuli and a trig point. Allow about 4¼ hours for the walk.
START Roadside parking at SO 061518, alongside the A481.

1 From the roadside parking area, head east for a short distance and go past the turning on the right for Aberedw Village. Continue to follow the verge of the main road for a few more yards to reach a lane descending to the right, near a post box (at the time of writing, this was out of use on account of being used by nesting birds!). Follow the lane downhill, going STRAIGHT AHEAD at the junction. Pass a second house on the right and go through a gate onto an enclosed track.

2 Follow the track uphill and then on a more level course. On reaching a fork in the track, head HALF RIGHT (through a gate with a 'Please Close' notice). Follow the track up the left hand side of the field. Pass through a further gate and continue along the left hand side of the next field. Pass through the remains of an old field boundary, indicated by trees, and soon join a farm access track. Follow this along the left hand side of the field and then round to the left.

3 Follow the track round to the right and through a gate onto the open access land, near a small quarry on the left. Bear HALF RIGHT on the now steep track – *this gives excellent views towards the Wye Valley and Builth Wells on the right, as well as across the valley to the Carneddau (the two hills to the left of this range are the sites of hill forts).* Follow the track through several bends, with the ascent gradually becoming easier. Pass a

small rock outcropping on the right and continue along the track to the brow of the hill, where there is a fork in the track.

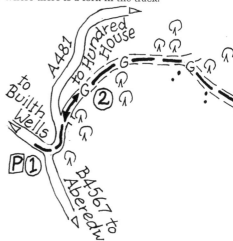

4 The most direct way to reach Black Rock Pools is to follow the left hand track, but for a more scenic route (looking across the valley to the Carneddau) turn SHARP LEFT and strike out along the high ground to the left of the direct track. After about half a mile, follow a track leading to the right to reach a junction of tracks to the east of Black Rock Pools.

5 Go STRAIGHT AHEAD over the junction of tracks or turn RIGHT if the grassy track has been followed from the top of Rhiw Rhwstyn. If following the latter route, it includes a right fork in the track just before the large second pool in the group. The trig point can be seen on the summit of the hill ahead and the course of the wide grassy track is also indicated by two white-topped posts (placed in connection with an annual horseriding event).

6 At a junction of tracks, just before a further white-topped pole, follow a grassy track past a pool. Go STRAIGHT AHEAD over a junction of tracks, heading uphill towards the trig point. Continue AHEAD until the trig point comes into view again. There is no 'main path' to reach this, so follow the track until quite close to the trig

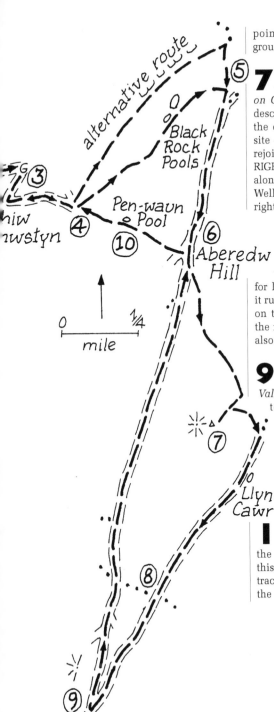

point and then strike out across the open ground on the right.

7 *There are a wide range of views here – including the neighbouring trig point on Garth, near Builth Wells.* When ready, descend from the trig point and head across the open ground to the next small rise (the site of a tumulus). Cross this and descend to rejoin the grassy track near Llyn Cawr. Turn RIGHT and follow the track past the lake and along the hill. Look out for a view of Builth Wells on the right – soon after this, take the right hand of two parallel tracks.

8 Pass a waymark post near enclosed fields on the left. Follow the right hand track up a slope, (passing the unexpected sight of a bath being used for livestock purposes!). Follow the track as it runs roughly parallel to the enclosed fields on the left. When nearing the place where the field boundary makes a turn to the right, also turn SHARP RIGHT onto a grassy track.

9 Follow this track back along the hill – *now with excellent views over the Wye Valley and the hills beyond.* Pass five white-topped poles on route. Shortly before reaching the sixth pole, cross over a junction of tracks. Almost immediately, bear HALF LEFT on a second track that leads past two ponds, both on the left. Join another track coming from the right and continue AHEAD over the brow of a hill.

10 Pass to the left of Pen-waun Pool and follow the track down to rejoin the Rhiw Rhwstyn. Turn LEFT and follow this back down the hill, fields and enclosed track to the lane. Follow the lane and then the road verge back to the parking area.

11

WYLFRE

DESCRIPTION This energetic 7 mile walk starts by following a short section of the River Edw, before taking one of the easier routes up to the Aberedw hills. After a section of lane, bridleways and then paths lead up to and round part of Wylfre, offering a wide range of views. A visit to the trig point on the top of the hill allows further views – particularly towards the south. The latter part of the walk continues along the high ground, passing hilltop pools, before returning via the Edw valley section. Allow about 4¼ hours for the walk.

START Car park at Hundred House, near Hundred House Inn, SO 113544.

PUBLIC TRANSPORT Powys Bus X11 (Mon & Thurs only) allows 5 hours for the walk. Bus stop is by car park at Hundred House.

1 From the car park, follow the main road to the Hundred House Inn. Cross the main road with care and go through the way-marked gate opposite. Cross a small field and go through a further gate. Head along the left hand side of the next, large, field to a footbridge. Cross and bear LEFT along a former streambed. After a while, follow the path up the bank on the right and bear LEFT, now to the right hand side of a fence. Cross a stile and head along the right hand side of the field for a short way to a waymarked gate on the right.

2 Go through this and follow a short section of track up between gorse bushes. At the top turn LEFT and follow a path running along the left hand side of the field to reach a waymarked gate onto a road. Turn LEFT on the road and follow this until reaching an unfenced lane on the right, marked as No Through Road. Follow the lane uphill and round to the right. Pass to the left of Graig-yr-onen and continue AHEAD up the stony track. When the stony track turns left through a gate, continue AHEAD to the right of the fence to reach another, waymarked, gate on the left.

3 Turn LEFT through the gate and very soon turn LEFT again on a slightly sunken grassy track. On reaching a junction with a stony track, near a bridleway sign, cross the stony track and continue AHEAD on a further section of grassy track. At the next junction of tracks, take the left fork which runs close to a fence on the left. When the fence bears left, follow this for another few yards. By a gate in the fence, bear HALF RIGHT on a grassy track through bracken. Bear LEFT at the junction with a wider track coming from the right.

4 Follow the track and then the path on a circuit around the left hand side of Wylfre – *for a range of excellent views.* On reaching an area of thicker gorse bushes, turn RIGHT and head up to the flat summit of the hill. Head for the trig point – *following a curving route towards this allows additional views.*

5 When ready, follow a path leading towards the western side of Wylfre. Follow the path down between gorse bushes and then through bracken, to meet a wider track near the corner of a fenceline. Several tracks meet here – with left shoulder towards the corner of the fenceline, take the third track from the left. Follow this towards the brow of the next hill and AHEAD to a junction of stony tracks by a bridleway sign.

6 Continue AHEAD on a rutted track just to the right of the bridleway sign. Pass to the right of an attractive pond. Look out for sight of conifers off to the right – having sighted these, continue until reaching a junction of tracks and then turn SHARP RIGHT. Bear RIGHT again at a junction with another track coming from the left. Follow the track running to the right of the conifers and then to the right of enclosed fields until reaching the gate passed through on the outward journey.

7 Go through the gate and follow the stony track and then lane down past Graig-yr-onen. Bear LEFT on the road. Follow the footpath on the right back along the field, descending to the gate in a dip. Head LEFT to the stile and follow the path through the woods to the footbridge. Head back along the two fields to reach the main road opposite the Hundred House Inn.

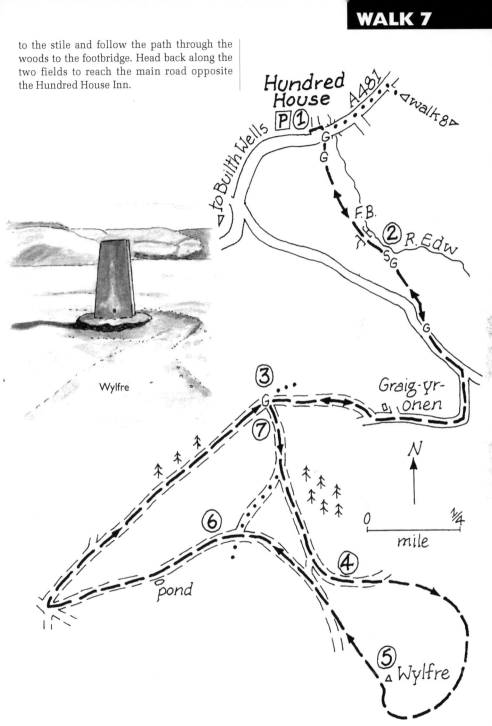

Hundred House

to Builth Wells

A481

◁walk 8▷

P ①

G

G

F.B.

② R. Edw

SG

G

③

G

Graig-yr-onen

⑦

N

0 ¼

mile

⑥

pond

④

⑤ Wylfre

Wylfre

WALK 8

GIANT'S GRAVE, LITTLE HILL & GLASCWM

DESCRIPTION Starting from near Hundred House Inn, this energetic 8½ mile route leads uphill by lane and track to the Giant's Grave tumulus on the ridge between Glascwm and Hundred House. Attractive valley views during the ascent lead to a panoramic sight of the Carneddau beyond Hundred House and Aberedw Hill off to the right. From the tumulus, a hill top track leads over heather moorland and past two ponds to join a quiet lane to Glascwm village, with views across the valley to Glascwm Hill on route. The final stage of the route follows another track up from Glascwm, along the side of a scenic valley, then back to Hundred House via the Giant's Grave. Allow about 4¾ hours for the walk.

START Car park at Hundred House, near Hundred House Inn, SO 113544.

PUBLIC TRANSPORT Powys Bus X11 (Builth Wells to Ludlow, Mon & Thurs only) allows 5 hours for the walk. Bus stop is by car park at Hundred House.

1 From the car park, head north past the Hundred House Inn (01982 570231). Follow the main road over the Edw Bridge. Take the second turn on the right, signposted for Rhiw Farm and as a no-through lane. Follow the lane uphill for about a mile – steeply in places – *but with good views back towards the Carneddau and Aberedw Hill.* At the end of the tarmac lane, continue AHEAD on the enclosed track, soon going through a gate onto open access land.

2 Follow the track ahead, with a fence to the left. When the fence bends sharp left, continue AHEAD across the open land to reach the Giant's Grave tumulus, with a waymark post nearby. On reaching the waymark post, turn sharp RIGHT and follow a grassy track up Little Hill. After about 100 yards, take the left fork in the track. Follow

the track across the heather moorland, passing between two waymark posts. At the next fork, keep to the main, right hand, track. Pass to the left of a hill top pond.

3 On meeting a second track coming from the right, just beyond a second pond, continue along the grassy track as this now descends and bears to the right. On nearing enclosed fields on the right, bear LEFT to reach an unfenced lane running along the lower edge of the open access land. Turn LEFT on the lane and follow this to a gate.

4 Go through the gate and follow the enclosed lane for about another half-mile. Just after crossing the Clas-Brook, turn RIGHT on a waymarked track. Follow this to

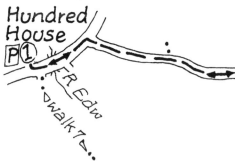

the junction with another lane – *at this point the house to be seen on the right (The Yat) is the former vicarage, now a guesthouse.* Turn LEFT and go through the gate into St David's churchyard. The use of 'clas' for the name of the nearby stream, as well as in the village name, indicates that this was religious settlement. When ready, exit by the gate at the far end of the churchyard. Follow the lane AHEAD into Glascwm, until reaching the junction by the phone box. The former village school, at one time a Youth Hostel, can be seen on the right as you approach the junction.

5 From the phone box, head down to the bridge over the Clas-Brook. Cross the bridge and continue straight AHEAD, passing through a gate across the lane. When the lane becomes a track, continue AHEAD on the main route, which skirts the attractive valley

Glascwm

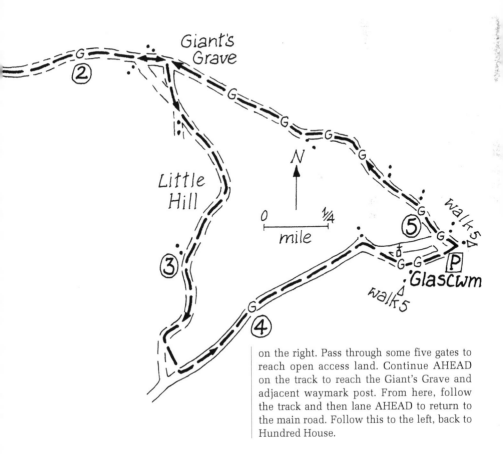

on the right. Pass through some five gates to reach open access land. Continue AHEAD on the track to reach the Giant's Grave and adjacent waymark post. From here, follow the track and then lane AHEAD to return to the main road. Follow this to the left, back to Hundred House.

WALK 9
MICHAELCHURCH-ON-ARROW & MILTON HILL

DESCRIPTION A moderate 4 mile walk, starting from St Michael's Church and following a lane and bridleway route to the open access land at Milton Hill. After crossing the hill, from where there are views towards Hergest Ridge and Disgwylfa Hill (both crossed by Offa's Dyke Path), the route follows two (mainly) unsurfaced highways (the second of which is a tree-lined path, fringed by a range of wild flowers in season). Returning to the open access land, the walk then follows a route designated as a 'byway open to all traffic' but in practice only used by horseriders and walkers, finally joining a lane route (partly along the course of the Welsh-English border) to return to Michaelchurch-on-Arrow. Allow about 2¼ hours for the walk.
START Limited parking near the church at SO 247507.

1 Facing the lane outside the church grounds, turn RIGHT and follow the lane for about half a mile to the houses at Milton. When the lane makes a turn to the right here, bear LEFT. Pass to the right of a house and look for a path leading off to the left, just after a caravan. Turn LEFT and follow the path past an old railway wagon and through a gate onto an enclosed track. Follow the track up to a further gate onto Milton Hill open access land.

2 Shortly after passing through the gate, take the right fork in the track. Very soon, bear HALF RIGHT on a path that runs roughly parallel to the field boundary on the right. Cross over a farm access track leading to a gate on the right. Continue to follow the path AHEAD for a few more yards, then bear RIGHT on a track that soon crosses a shallow ford. After another few yards, take the left fork in the track.

3 Follow the grassy track uphill and then gradually round to the right. On reaching a clearing in the bracken, maintain direction slightly to the right, soon rejoining a grassy track. Bear LEFT at the next fork in the track, soon crossing the brow of the hill. Pass between enclosed fields, following a route that passes close to the corner of the field boundary on the left. Continue AHEAD on a grassy track that leads to the edge of the open access land. Join a stony track and turn LEFT on this to pass through a gate onto an enclosed track.

4 Go STRAIGHT AHEAD on the enclosed track until reaching the junction with a lane. Turn SHARP LEFT and join a path waymarked as a 'public road'. At the far end of this, go through a gate back onto the open access land. Turn RIGHT and follow the boundary of the open access land. On reaching the eastern boundary of Milton Hill, go through a small gate and follow a path along an enclosed grassy strip of land.

5 Pass through an old gateway into a narrow field and continue AHEAD on a faint path which runs along the right hand side of the field. On nearing Trenewydd, go through a gate onto an enclosed track. Follow this to the junction with a lane, and bear LEFT on this. At the crossroads, turn LEFT. Follow the lane past the open access sections at Brilley Mountain and round to the left.

6 On reaching a junction signposted for 'Huntington' turn RIGHT and follow the lane until just beyond The Gaer (on the right). After a few yards, turn SHARP LEFT onto an enclosed track. Cross a small stream and continue along the track, being joined by another track coming from the right. Pass in sight of a shed, off to the right, and soon join a lane. Turn RIGHT to return to the church.

to **Milton**

16

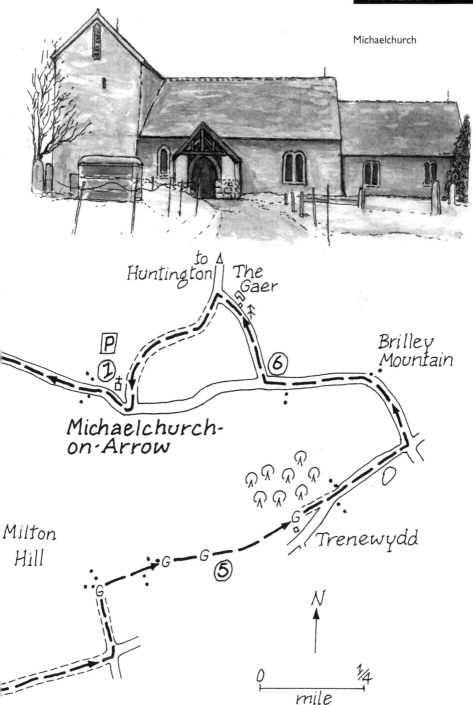

Michaelchurch

to Huntington

The Gaer

Brilley Mountain

P

1

Michaelchurch-on-Arrow

6

Trenewydd

Milton Hill

G — G

5

G

N

0 ¼ mile

ABEREDW VALLEY WALK

DESCRIPTION A river valley walk with the option of two lengths – 3¾ miles (easy) or 5¾ miles (moderate). Starting from near a riverside picnic area, the route follows a lane into Aberedw village, with its castle site, church and adjacent public house, before heading for a riverside footpath. Passing alternately through oak woods and across meadows, this leads to a lane junction near a bridge – from here the easy route option leads by lane back to the picnic area. The moderate option continues to follow a footpath via fields and woods, before climbing to join an unsurfaced highway. The final stretch of the moderate route follows a lane, from which there are excellent views on both sides. Allow 2 or 3 hours, depending on length of route selected, plus time to visit the pub and sights on route. As the riverside paths can be muddy, this route has been planned to cover the drier sections first, for the benefit of walkers planning to call at the pub.

START Riverside picnic area on lane leading east from Aberedw village, SO 102482. Leave the B4567 at the turning for Aberedw village (SO 076475). Go through the village, passing the Seven Stars public house and the church, on the right. Descend the hill and take the right fork at the phone box. At the next junction, take the left fork and follow the riverside lane over a cattlegrid and continue to the parking area near the riverside picnic benches.

1 From the picnic area, retrace the outward route back to the village. On reaching St Cewydd's church, turn LEFT into the churchyard. The site of Aberedw Castle can be reached by crossing a stile on the far side of the churchyard and heading RIGHT along the field. The mound will be seen on the left. When ready, retrace the route through the churchyard and turn LEFT to reach the Severn Stars. The name relates to the stars in the Virgin Mary's Crown and indicates that the church once owned the pub.

2 When ready, retrace the route east from the village, going RIGHT at the fork in the lane by the phone box. Just before reaching the first bridge, turn LEFT over the waymarked stile. Head along the field to reach a waymarked stile into oak woodland. Continue AHEAD on a path running to the left of the fence and the River Edw, soon being joined by the track coming from the left. Cross a cleared area, keeping roughly parallel to the river.

3 At the far side of the clearing, rejoin the track for a short climb back into woodland. On leaving the woodland, continue

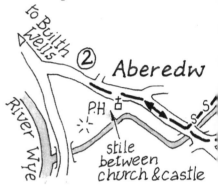

along the field, keeping close to the river. (On this section, keep an eye out for a house on the other side of the river – the partial remains of a footbridge can be seen). Pass through a gap between fences. Ignore a track leading off to the left and continue AHEAD along the field. At the far end of the field, bear SLIGHTLY TO THE LEFT (there is a waymark sign on the fence to the right at this point). Keep to the left of the fence to reach a stile in the far corner of the field, leading to a lane.

4 Turn RIGHT on the lane and follow this round to the right to reach a bridge over the River Edw. *For the easy option, cross the bridge and turn LEFT. Follow the lane back to the picnic area.* For the moderate walk option, cross the waymarked footbridge on the left, just before the main bridge. Go along the field for a few yards to a further

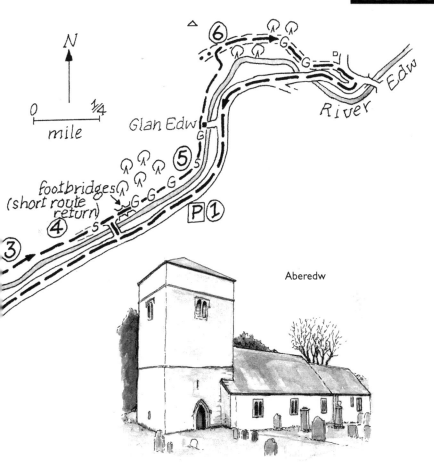

Aberedw

footbridge. Cross and head HALF RIGHT to a waymarked gate to the right of an old shed. Continue along the next field to a waymarked gate in the far right corner. Follow the path through the wood – this is faint in places, but stays fairly close to the river and soon has a fence to its right. Go through a further way-marked gate and continue AHEAD, to the left of the fence. Pass an old ford and a group of trees to reach a stile in the field corner near the river.

5 Head along the next field, towards Glan Edw farm. On nearing the buildings, bear HALF LEFT. Go through a gate to the left of the farm enclosure. Head diagonally HALF LEFT across the next field, climbing gradually up the hill. The higher sections of

a field boundary have been removed, so pass to the left of what remains of the fence and continue to head HALF LEFT up the field, until reaching an old trackway running along the top of the field.

6 Turn RIGHT and follow the trackway through the wood and then downhill to a gate. Continue AHEAD on the track through the trees, to the right of a field. On leaving the trees, continue to follow the track across a field to the riverside. Go through a further gate and continue along the track for a short way to reach a junction with a lane, near a house on the left. Turn RIGHT and follow the lane over the Edw and back to the riverside picnic area.

ABEREDW ROCKS & WYESIDE PATH

DESCRIPTION Starting with a climb to a hilltop from where there are excellent views over the Wye Valley, this energetic walk of some 5¾ miles goes on to explore the dramatic outcroppings of Aberedw Rocks. The later stages of the walk provide a complete contrast, using a riverside footpath to return to the Craft Centre, where light refreshments are available, as well as a wide range of arts, crafts and books of local interest. Allow about 3 hours for the walk.

START Erwood Old Station Craft Centre Car Park, SO 089439.

PUBLIC TRANSPORT Powys Bus 704 (Newtown to Brecon), operates via A470, on the other side of the Wye from the Craft Centre (alight Erwood Bridge and follow Wye Valley Walk signs across river).

I From the Craft Centre car park, cross the adjacent B-road with care and start up the no-through lane opposite. At the top of the triangle of grass on the right, turn LEFT onto a path up through bracken. Follow this uphill, being joined by another path from the right, to reach Garreg Fawr with its excellent viewpoint over the Wye Valley. Continue over the brow of the hill and take the left fork in the path. Follow a grassy track between areas of bracken, to the left of enclosed fields. Follow the fence round to the right, cross a further outcropping and continue to the left of the fence. Descend on a path (fairly steep in places) to an unfenced lane.

2 Turn RIGHT and follow the lane uphill and round to the right. On reaching the second grit container, on the right, turn LEFT. Take the left hand track. On sighting fields, on the right, aim HALF LEFT and soon go LEFT again, across the top of a valley to the left. After a few more yards, take the right fork in the track. Pass to the left and then to the right of rock outcroppings. Cross the brow of the hill and follow the track AHEAD towards Aberedw Rocks, now clearly visible ahead.

3 Follow sheep paths up and across the top of the first section of the rocks, allowing further views across the Wye Valley. Descend to a track that runs between two sections of the Rocks. Turn RIGHT and very soon turn LEFT on a grassy path that runs along the base of the rocks. Ignore the first path leading up onto the rocks and continue until reaching a grassy track leading half left uphill. Follow this over the brow of the hill and then downwards towards the Wye Valley. In due course, follow the track round to the right (roughly parallel to the Wye Valley), descend a slope and continue AHEAD on the path. Descend a second slope and continue HALF RIGHT to reach the remains of an old stone wall.

4 Turn SHARP LEFT at the remains of the old wall. Follow a path past an outcropping on the left. Continue AHEAD on the path, which descends and then bears left alongside a field boundary. Take the left fork in the path, passing to the right of rock outcroppings, then bear LEFT and follow the path which runs roughly parallel to the base of the rocks until reaching a gap in the rocks near which is a small boundary stone.

5 Turn RIGHT at this point and follow a track past further rocks. At a junction of tracks, by a pond, turn SHARP LEFT. Head along a grassy area and cross a concrete 'step'. Follow the path AHEAD along a small valley. When the path leaves the valley, bear HALF LEFT on a side path. After a few yards, take the right fork in the path and follow this down to the unfenced lane.

6 Cross the lane and continue AHEAD up the steep path to the right of the field boundary. Follow this uphill and past a small rock outcropping. When the field boundary makes a sharp turn to the left, turn RIGHT and follow a grassy track running downhill towards houses. On reaching a tarmac lane, turn LEFT. Almost immediately, turn RIGHT over the cattlegrid. Follow the road past the remains of a railway bridge, until reaching a turning on the left opposite Wyeside house. Turn LEFT and cross the cattlegrid, adjacent to which are waymark signs.

7 Follow a waymark sign (on a tree) HALF LEFT across the field. Go through a gap in the trees and head HALF RIGHT to a gate. Go through and follow the path to the left. Descend steps and continue LEFT on the riverside path, passing through two gates. Follow the path to the left of wooden railings and cross a footbridge. Continue to follow the path as it runs to the left of a fence and then between fences to another gate. Go through and follow the path to the left of a fence, to reach a gate on the left to the Craft Centre.

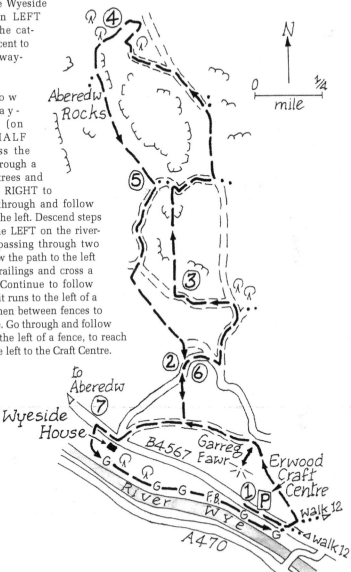

N

0   1/4
mile

Aberedw
Rocks

to
Aberedw

Wyeside
House

B4567

Garreg
Fawr

Erwood
Craft
Centre

River Wye

F.B.

A470

walk 12

walk 12

WALK 12

THE SKREEN & TWYN Y GARTH

DESCRIPTION An energetic walk of approximately 4 miles, exploring a wooded dingle and crossing the first area of open access land to join an old unsurfaced highway. Passing fields and woodland, the route then joins paths and a track leading up the summit of Twyn y Garth, with the unexpected sight of a hilltop cannon. A walk around the eastern half of the hill leads back to the outward track that is followed to the junction with a road near Erwood Craft Centre. Allow about 2½ hours for the walk.
START Erwood Old Station Car Park, SO 089439
PUBLIC TRANSPORT Powys Bus 704 (Newtown to Brecon), operates via the A470, just across the Erwood Bridge from the Craft Centre.

1 Cross the adjacent B-road and turn RIGHT. In a few yards, turn LEFT and follow the steep lane up past the house on the right. Continue AHEAD on the lane, which soon becomes a dirt track. On nearing the point where the lane bends to the left and heads for Nelfa, look for a path leading down into the wooded dingle on the right.

2 Follow the path down into the wood. Bear RIGHT, crossing a shallow stream. Take the right hand path, leading above the stream. Cross a second shallow stream and follow a path that now begins to ascend. Take the right hand fork in the path, soon emerging from the woods. Continue downhill to the unfenced road.

3 Cross the road and head along the open ground of the Skreen, above Sunnybank Cottages. Cross the brow of a small rise and take a diagonal course HALF RIGHT down the hill, through the bracken. A track runs along the base of this small area of open

access land – a line of three telegraph poles at the lower edge of the Skreen also make a good visual reference point to aim for.

4 Turn LEFT and follow the track along the base of the open access land. Go through an old gateway and follow the track between fences, along the base of woodland. Cross a shallow stream and continue along the track. Cross old sheep hurdles into Twyn y Garth open access area.

5 Turn SHARP LEFT and follow a steep path for some way up the left hand boundary of the open access area. On reaching piles of stones, on the right, bear RIGHT on a track leading around the shoulder of the hill. At a junction of routes, bear HALF LEFT on a path towards a nearby rock. On reaching the rock, turn LEFT and follow a path running uphill through bracken. Follow this to the cannon, a short way beyond which are the earthworks and extensive views.

6 When ready, return to the cannon and follow a path leading off to the left. Soon take the left fork and follow a wide grassy track along the hill and then downwards towards enclosed fields near New Gardens. At the edge of the open access land, turn RIGHT and follow a path along its edge until reaching a stile on the left.

7 Cross the stile and head HALF RIGHT across the field until reaching the line of a track running along the edge of the field. Turn RIGHT and follow this to the gate into Twyn y Garth (the apparent shorter option of continuing to descend within Twyn y Garth, although possible, is difficult going in places). Follow the track along the base of Twyn y Garth. Cross the sheep hurdles and continue along the track through the wood and along the base of the Skreen. At the junction with the lane, bear RIGHT. Go LEFT at the next junction. Continue past the turning on the left, leading to the Wye Bridge, to return to the Craft Centre.

Old signal box at Erwood Craft Centre

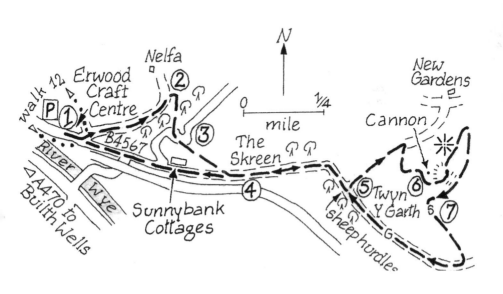

WALK 13
LLANSTEPHAN CIRCULAR

DESCRIPTION A choice between an easy route of some 1¾ miles and a moderate route of about 3¾ miles. The short route follows a riverside section of the Wye Valley Walk, then a footpath and old trackway across fields. The longer route also starts on the Wye Valley Walk, then follows an attractive lane route to St Stephan's Church. From here, the moderate route also follows an old trackway between fields, through woodland and across further fields. Both routes then lead down through a further short stretch of woodland to return to the Wye Valley Walk.

START Roadside parking near Wye Valley Walk sign at SO 106428. There are other lay-bys at various places on the same lane if the nearest two are unavailable.

PUBLIC TRANSPORT Powys Bus 704 (Newtown to Brecon) operates via the A470, on the other side of the River Wye. Llanstephan Bridge, near Trericket Mill, is the nearest crossing point.

1 BOTH ROUTES From the roadside parking, cross the Wye Valley Walk stile and descend the steps. Follow the path to the right, passing under the bridge supports. Cross a footbridge and bear HALF RIGHT to a gate onto a track. Follow the track along through the woodland (and often in sight of the Wye), passing through a further two gates. Near the end of the track, go through a further gate and turn RIGHT on the lane.

2 SHORT OPTION/EASY ROUTE Follow the lane for a short way until reaching the turning on the left for Cwrt y Graban. Head up the access route towards the house. Shortly before reaching the property, turn LEFT through a waymarked gate. Cross the field to a further gate. Continue AHEAD past a farm building and follow the track along the field. At a junction in the track, take the left fork. On nearing a gate into woodland, do not go through this, but turn SHARP LEFT. Follow stage 3 of the directions from this point.

LONGER OPTION/MODERATE ROUTE

A) Follow the lane past the turning on the right for Llanstephan Bridge. Follow the lane through parkland, with a view of Llanstephan House off to the left. Turn LEFT at the junction, signed for Llanstephan Church. Head up the hill and go RIGHT at the next junction. Continue up the hill, ignoring the next turn to the left. Pass a side turning on the right for The Flawdd. At the next two junctions, turn LEFT, following signposts for Llanstephan Church.

B) After a visit to the church, exit via the lychgate and turn LEFT on the enclosed track. At a junction of tracks, take the left fork and descend into woodland. Ignore a gate on the left and continue AHEAD to the next junction. Go STRAIGHT AHEAD (fire warning sign on right). Leave the far side of the wood via a gate and follow a faint track across the narrow field to another gate. Head HALF LEFT across the next field, to a gate to the left of trees, passing telegraph poles on route. Ignore the track ahead and bear slightly to the RIGHT, then keep roughly parallel to the enclosed wood on the right, until reaching a gate into woodland. Don't go through this, but maintain your direction roughly parallel to the enclosed wood.

3 BOTH ROUTES Keep roughly parallel to the enclosed wood on the right, passing a row of oaks also to the right. Follow a path through a small clump of oaks and join a track descending half right into woodland. Follow this downhill and go through a gate. Continue AHEAD for a short distance to the footbridge crossed in stage 1 above. Turn RIGHT over this and follow the path under the bridge supports and up the bank. Turn LEFT over the waymarked stile to return to the lane.

St Stephan's Church

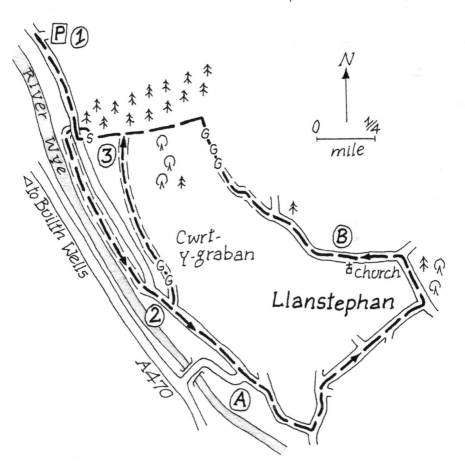

LLANDEILO HILL

DESCRIPTION A moderate 5½ mile hill walk with a range of excellent views, including of lakes, ponds and unusual rock outcroppings (Cradle Rocks). This route also passes Twm Tobacco's Grave, a memorial to a 'packman' (travelling pedlar) who died while crossing the hill. The northern section of the walk gives views towards the Edw valley. Allow about 3¾ hours for the walk.

START Roadside parking at SO 105456, alongside the Llandeilo Graban to Llanbedr road.

1 Starting from the western edge of the open access land (not far from the cattlegrid) follow a grassy track running north, close to the field boundary on the left. When the fence makes a sharp turn to the left, continue AHEAD across a small stream and take the first grassy track heading half right. At a junction of tracks, maintain direction, keeping to the right of the hawthorn trees. Pass through a gap near the end of the trees. After a few feet, turn RIGHT on a grassy track.

2 At the junction with a second grassy track, turn LEFT and head uphill. Join a stony track and continue to follow this uphill. At the brow of the hill there are good views of Llan Bwch-llyn (to the right) and soon Henllyn (to the left).

3 Pass to the right of Henllyn. Follow the track round to the right, along the top of a small escarpment. Look out for a further view of Llan Bwch-llyn – just after this passes out of sight, bear HALF RIGHT on a narrow path leading towards higher ground (hoofprints indicate that this route is used by horse riders). At a junction of tracks, continue AHEAD on a now wider grassy track, that soon follows the edge of a valley on the right.

4 Follow the track past two small but interestingly shaped rock outcroppings (on right and then on left). When the route becomes a faint path, maintain direction roughly parallel to the valley on the right. Pass a third rock outcrop and soon after turn RIGHT on a wide track (a fourth outcrop is visible off to the left).

5 Follow the track, which runs along the northern side of the open access area and gradually bears round to the right. Pass the turning for Cwm Iago (rock escarpment) off to the right. Continue AHEAD on the main track, crossing a shallow stream. Descend towards a dip in the ground, where there is a junction of several tracks – before reaching this turn LEFT and follow a grassy track that leads to the small lake at the foot of Garreg Lwyd.

6 Follow the path that runs up the left hand side of Garreg Lwyd. On reaching the crest of the hill, bear HALF LEFT on sheep paths through the low-growing heather, to return to the outward track. Turn RIGHT and follow the track back across the small stream to Cwm Iago (a detour could be made around this, using the path at the base, turning RIGHT at the end of the rocks and turning RIGHT again to follow further sheep paths back to the main track).

7 Continue along the track. At a junction of tracks, take the right fork, running roughly parallel to fields on the right. At a further junction, take the left fork in the track. Pass Twm Tobacco's Grave and the boundary stone just beyond this, both on the right. Continue AHEAD, with a view of Henllyn off to the left. Pass through a line of grouse butts and follow the left hand track AHEAD, soon passing Glannau Pool, on the left.

8 At a junction of tracks, head HALF LEFT. On nearing a sizeable number of hawthorn trees, again take the left hand track and follow this round to the left. Cross a clearing and continue AHEAD through further trees. Cross two small streams and follow a track running half right to the field boundary. Turn LEFT and follow the field boundary back to the unfenced lane.

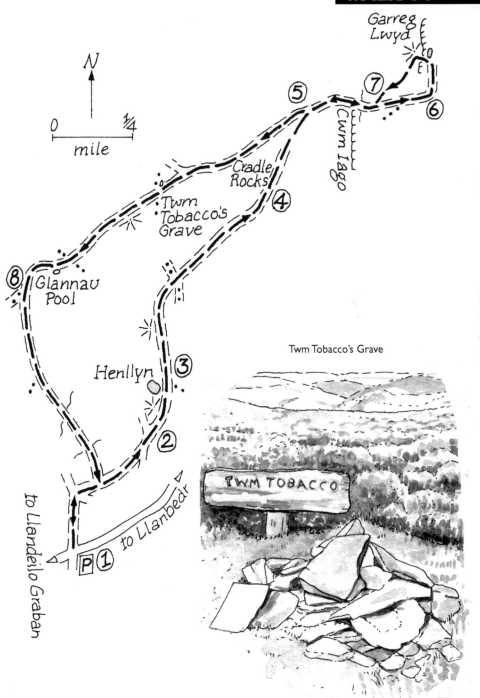

N

0 ¼
mile

Garreg
Lwyd

⑤

⑦

⑥

Cwm Iago

Cradle
Rocks

⑧ Glannau
Pool

·Twm
·Tobacco's
Grave

④

Henllyn

③

②

to Llandeilo Graban

to Llanbedr

P ①

Twm Tobacco's Grave

TWM TOBACCO

27

RHULEN HILL

DESCRIPTION This moderate 3½ mile walk follows tracks across open access land, visiting hill top lakes and ponds and passing in sight of attractive rock outcroppings. There are also excellent views to the south (Begwns, Black Mountains and Brecon Beacons) and north towards Glascwm Hill and across the Edw valley. Allow about 2 hours for the walk.

START Roadside near Ireland, at SO 147484, between Painscastle and Rhulen.

1 Follow the road towards Painscastle for a few yards. Ignore the path on the right, alongside the stream. Take the next track on the right. Follow the track as it skirts round to the left of Llyn y March (lake). Continue to follow the track past a large area of heather – once beyond this, head HALF LEFT on a path that soon leads to the junction with a second path.

2 Turn LEFT on the second path, which soon shows evidence of greater use. At a junction of tracks, head RIGHT, following a grassy track ahead and then round to the right above fields, with a view of the Begwns beyond. At a junction of tracks near a field boundary, turn RIGHT on a grassy track.

3 Cross over a junction of tracks, maintaining direction diagonally up the hill and soon following a slightly sunken track. Pass in sight of a small disused quarry some way off to the right. At a further junction of tracks, follow the slightly sunken track leading half left. At hill top, turn LEFT on a stony track that provides views of a number of small lakes and pools off to the right, Garreg Lwyd outcropping (also on the right) and Craig y Fuddal to the left. On nearing the outcroppings, follow the track down to the lowest point and turn SHARP RIGHT.

4 Follow a rutted track heading left at an angle of about 45° from the outward route. Follow the track across fairly level ground to the south of Rhulen Hill, passing to the left of an upland lake (Mawn Pool). Eventually descend on a grassy track through heather and past a group of trees. On reaching two enclosed fields, follow the track between these.

Walk 14

5 Continue down towards the unfenced road now visible ahead. Shortly before reaching this, turn SHARP RIGHT and follow a grassy track over the brow of the hill and AHEAD to the road. Turn RIGHT and follow the road back to the parking area.

Mawn Pool

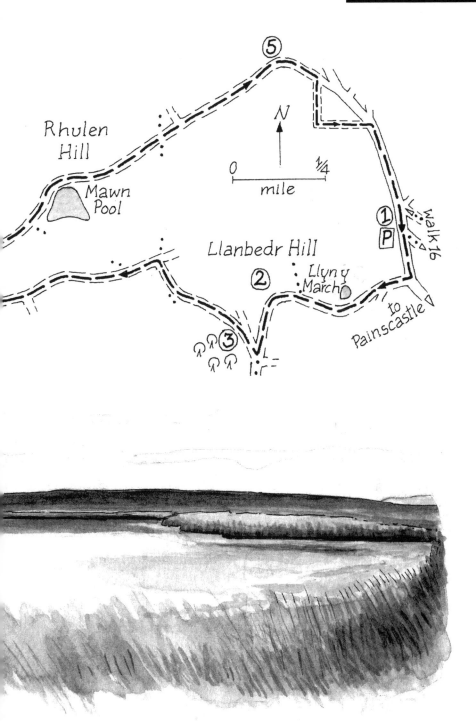

PAINSCASTLE

DESCRIPTION From the Roast Ox Inn (where an old well can be seen inside the public house), this moderate walk of about 4¼ miles starts with a climb to open access land on the hill above Painscastle village. The circular route takes in extensive views, including south towards the Black Mountains and north towards Glascwm Hill. In addition to the well in the pub, there is another well in a small public garden area a short distance away in the village. Allow about 2½ hours for the walk.

START Parking area outside the Roast Ox Inn (please phone 01497 851398 to ask first), SO 167464.

I Take the lane running uphill to the left of the Roast Ox, passing a chapel on the right. Continue on the lane until crossing a cattlegrid. Almost immediately, bear HALF RIGHT on a track running uphill. At the fork, take the grassy left hand track. On nearing the field boundary, bear HALF RIGHT to return to the main track.

2 Follow the main track to the left for a short way, then bear LEFT on a grassy track running between areas of bracken. Follow the main track across the brow of the hill. When the track becomes faint, bear SLIGHTLY TO THE RIGHT, passing between areas of low growing gorse. On the far side of the gorse bushes, maintain direction, keeping roughly parallel to enclosed fields on the right.

3 On meeting a stony track near the corner of a field, bear LEFT on this. In a few yards, bear LEFT again on a grassy track leading towards the left hand end of a row of trees. Cross a small stream and immediately bear HALF LEFT on a grassy track running towards the right shoulder of the hill ahead. Follow the track for about 1 mile, passing close to the enclosed fields at Ireland.

4 On reaching the unfenced lane, turn LEFT and walk parallel to this. When the ground becomes overgrown/damp, follow the lane. At the junction, take the left fork and follow this down to the cattlegrid and then down the enclosed lane back to Painscastle.

N

0 ¼
mile

③

②

P ①
Roast Ox
Inn

Painscastle

B4594

B4594 to
Builth Wells

RHOSGOCH COMMON

DESCRIPTION A 4½ mile walk, starting from Rhosgoch village. This route combines lanes and an old trackway, both of which give views towards the National Nature Reserve at Rhosgoch Common (a wetland reserve including wet woodland, transition mires, bog and quaking bog). Readers of Kilvert's Diary will find other features of interest – the site of Rhosgoch Mill, the farmhouse formerly belonging to the Nonconformist Minister 'Griffiths of Portway' and the nearby chapel. The walk passes the start of an entrance route to Rhosgoch Common itself – *however please note that the Nature Conservancy Council Wales have advised that visitors should only enter the Common in groups, for safety reasons. Visitors should also familiarise themselves with the information on the board near the entry gate, and come equipped with suitable footwear and equipment (e.g. walking poles to test the ground before stepping on this). Please note that there is no set path and not all parts of the Common are safe for walkers. WALKERS ARE REMINDED THAT THEY ENTER THE COMMON AT THEIR OWN RISK.* Allow about 2¾ hours for the walk.

START Roadside parking, Rhosgoch village, SO 186477.

1 Facing the road outside the chapel, turn RIGHT and follow the B4594 for a short way to see the former mill at Rhosgoch (mentioned in Kilvert's Diary). When ready, return to the junction near the chapel and turn RIGHT. At the next junction, turn LEFT into a lane. Follow the lane towards the B4594, looking out for a track leading off between two houses on the right. *This track leads to the entrance to the Common – please note the safety information above and on the information board by the gate.* When ready return to the lane and turn RIGHT. On reaching the junction with the B road, turn RIGHT.

2 Follow the B road past a turning on the left. Shortly afterwards, look for the white farmhouse on the left – this is the home of the 'Griffiths of Portway' mentioned above. Shortly after this, as the road begins to climb, field gates on the right allow views towards Rhosgoch Common (NB no rights of way exist from the road). Go past the entrance to a second lane on the left to reach a crossroads, with a phone box nearby.

3 Turn RIGHT here and follow the lane down and then uphill to the junction near Newgate. Turn RIGHT on a narrow lane and shortly turn RIGHT again. Go past a house on the right. Pass an old barn and shortly afterwards go through a gate with a clearly visible track beyond (just before reaching a new house on the right).

4 Follow the left hand boundary of three fields, connected by gates. At the end of the third field, go through the right hand gate and pass through a small wood. Towards the far side of this, walk between fences. Continue along the left hand side of the next field to reach a further gate. Cross a small stream and head along the middle of the field, keeping to the left of the rough ground to reach a gate, beyond which Rhosgoch Golf Club clubhouse can be seen.

5 Go through the gate and follow a clear track across the golf course to meet an access road near the car park. Follow the access road over a cattlegrid and continue AHEAD to reach the junction with a lane. Turn RIGHT and take the left fork at the next junction to return to the chapel.

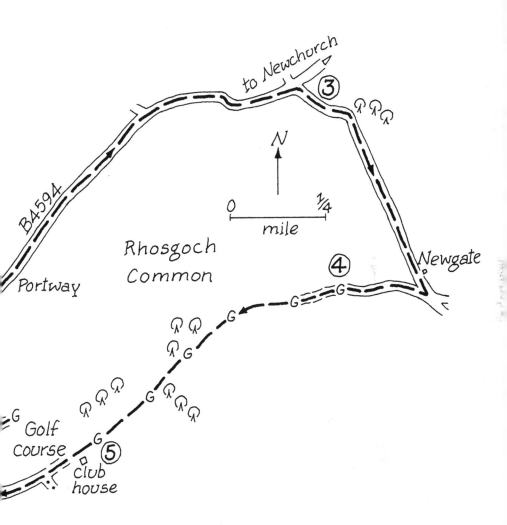

to Newchurch

③

N

0 — ¼
mile

B4594

Portway

Rhosgoch
Common

④

Newgate

G

Golf
Course

⑤
Club
house

33

HOLY WELL WALK

DESCRIPTION This generally easy walk of some 4¾ miles (with one ascent) starts and ends alongside the River Wye. After following part of the Wye Valley Walk across fields, it joins a lane and footpath route via an historic local chapel to the village of Ffynnon Gynydd, the site of the Holy Well of the title. The rest of the route heads across Ffynnon Gynydd Common and descends through Fishpond Wood. After following the B road back towards Glasbury, a diversion leads past attractive houses to an open access area alongside the Wye near Glasbury Bridge. Allow about 2¾ hours for the walk.

START Parking area to the north of Glasbury Bridge, alongside B4350. SO 178393.

PUBLIC TRANSPORT Powys Bus 39 (Brecon to Hereford via Hay-on-Wye), passes just to the south of Glasbury Bridge.

I From the parking area, head to the nearby junction with the A438. Cross the main road with care and descend the steps by the Wye Valley Walk waymark sign. Go through the kissing gate and head along the right hand side of the field. Keep to the right of the high fence and go through a second kissing gate. Continue along the right hand side of the fields, passing through another two kissing gates. Continue along a further field until reaching a Wye Valley Walk waymark post. Bear half left across the field at this point, aiming for the next waymark post. Cross a track by means of two kissing gates, then cross the narrow field to a final kissing gate onto the A438.

2 Cross the main road with care (fast traffic but good visibility at this point). Head right along the verge for a few yards, then turn left on the lane signposted 'Capel Maesyronnen Chapel ½'. Follow the lane past the attractive buildings at Glanhenwye (on the right) and the gatehouse to Maesllwch Castle (on the left). Follow the lane uphill (it is worth pausing to look back across the

Wye Valley to the Black Mountains) and past Maesyronnen farm. Follow the lane for a short way further, then turn RIGHT on the lane signposted for Maesyronnen Chapel. Built in approximately 1696, this is an attractively white painted building, with slate roof, said to be one of the oldest Non-Conformist chapels in Wales.

3 Facing the chapel, turn left and head for a stile to the left of a gate. Follow a path along the right hand side of the field to a further stile. Cross and turn RIGHT on the lane. Follow this to the village of Ffynnon Gynydd, ignoring a waymark post on the right on route. On reaching the junction in the village, turn RIGHT and follow the lane for a short way to the covered well on the left. Although the well is not available for drinking purposes, the shelter contains an inscription, together with two seats.

4 When ready, return to the junction and turn RIGHT. Cross the cattlegrid and continue along the lane until reaching the waymark post on the left. Turn LEFT and follow the lane past the school. Shortly before reaching the end of the tarmac, near Oaklea, bear HALF RIGHT on a grassy track running across the Common. Pass through a gap in gorse bushes, at which point the Black Mountains come back into view. Head across the Common, joining a path that leads towards the right hand corner of the trees visible on the far side.

5 On reaching the trees, follow the path running just to their right, passing a waymark post on route. Descend through the wood, passing to the right of a house. Continue on the path, passing through a kissing gate into Fishpond Wood. On nearing Cwmbach, follow the path round to the right, through another kissing gate and over a footbridge to the road. Turn LEFT and follow the road towards Glasbury.

6 On reaching the Maesllwch Arms Hotel (01497 847637) cross the road and go past the railings into the lane opposite. Follow the lane for a short way to a green near a chapel (also with an attractive red

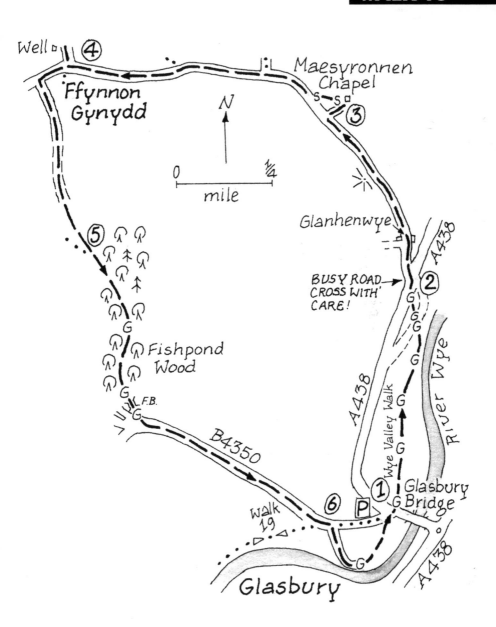

brick house to the right). Bear HALF RIGHT on the no-through lane, following this round to the left, passing a number of attractive houses. At the end of the lane, go through a gate and continue AHEAD to reach an open grassy area alongside the Wye. Head LEFT on a riverside path that leads towards Glasbury Bridge. On reaching the bridge, turn LEFT again, going through a final kissing gate to return to the parking area.

WYE VALLEY MEANDER I

DESCRIPTION An easy walk of about 3½ miles following the Wye Valley Walk alongside the river and across fields. The return journey uses an alternative footpath running alongside the Wye for much of its route. Allow about 2 hours for the walk.

START Parking area to the north of Glasbury Bridge, alongside B4350. SO 178393.

PUBLIC TRANSPORT Powys Bus 39 (Brecon to Hereford via Hay-on-Wye), passes just to the north of Glasbury Bridge.

1 Follow the road towards Cwmbach, passing the Maesllwch Arms Hotel on the right. When the road bends to the right, opposite the entrance to Glanrhyd/Brookside, cross the road to reach the Wye Valley Walk waymark post opposite. Follow a short section of track and go through a waymarked gate. Follow the track alongside the fence on the right and then continue AHEAD across the field to reach a concrete track near a waymark post.

2 Turn LEFT and follow the concrete track through a gate. Continue AHEAD on the track for some way until nearing Glasbury Farm. Go through a gate and continue AHEAD past the farmhouse, passing through another three gates on the far side. Follow the track AHEAD for a short way and then bear HALF LEFT on a grassy track running between trees and a hedge.

3 At the end of the trees and hedge, continue along the right hand side of the field to pass through a gate at the far end. Continue along the right hand side of the next field until reaching a gate on the right leading onto an enclosed track. Go through the gate and continue AHEAD along the track. Pass through a further gate and head HALF LEFT on an enclosed track. Ignore the Wye Valley Walk waymark post on the right and continue to follow the track, which now bends round to the left.

4 Pass Appleby, on the left. Shortly afterwards, go through the right hand of two gates on the left. Head along the left hand side of the field, then go LEFT over a footbridge. Continue AHEAD, following the remains of an old field boundary on the left. On nearing a pond, go through a gate to the left of this.

5 Head DIAGONALLY across this large field, passing the remains of an old field boundary on route, to reach a stile in the far right corner near the river. Cross and follow the right hand side of the field to a further stile. Enter the third, now very large, field (field boundaries have been removed) and continue to follow the right hand boundary alongside the river.

6 Cross a further stile (now level with Glasbury Farm). Continue to follow a riverside route, which gradually bends round to the left to meet the track followed on the outward journey. Turn RIGHT on this and follow it back to the gate onto the concrete track. Follow this track for a little way, then bear HALF RIGHT on the track across the field to the gate onto the enclosed track. Follow this to the road and then turn RIGHT to return to Glasbury Bridge.

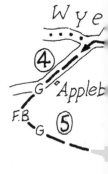

Glasbury

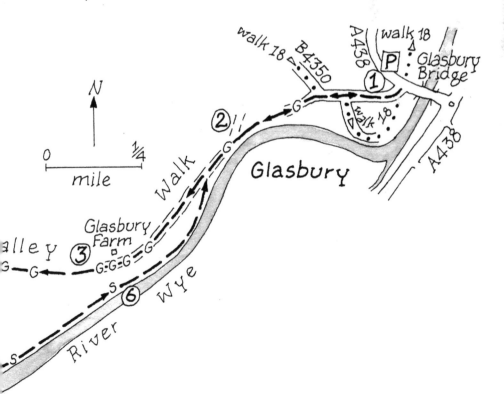

WYE VALLEY MEANDER 2

DESCRIPTION An easy 6½ mile walk along both sides of the River Wye, near Hay-on-Wye (the Town of Books nestling at the foot of the Black Mountains). This route uses a stretch of the Wye Valley Walk ('there-and-back-again') with access to the riverbank. The section of the walk on the other side of the river visits The Warren, a green area owned by Hay Warren Trustees. Allow about 3¾ hours for the walk.
START Hay-on-Wye Clock Tower, SO 229424.

I From the base of the Clock Tower, cross the main road and turn RIGHT. Head along the pavement to the turning on the left for Clyro. Follow this road over the Wye Bridge and continue on an uphill section until reaching a Wye Valley Walk waymark post on the left side of the road. Cross with care and go through a gate. Follow the path along the right hand edge of the field to a small gate in the far corner. Pass through and follow the waymarked path AHEAD for a few feet and then round to the RIGHT. Descend, with a wall on the right. Bypass an old stile and head HALF RIGHT for a few yards to cross a footbridge.

2 Turn LEFT on the track. On nearing the house, bear RIGHT on a grassy path running along the edge of the field. Follow the riverside path along arable fields, connected by gaps. On reaching the point where the Wye Valley Walk heads right towards the road, turn and retrace the outward route to the Clyro road. On returning to the Clyro road, head back down to the Wye Bridge.

3 Cross the bridge and immediately turn LEFT, following the waymarked route of the Wye Valley Walk down past the picnic area to the river. Bear LEFT, passing under the bridge and immediately head HALF RIGHT to pass through a small gate onto a path (i.e. the lower path by the river rather than the one shared with cyclists). Follow

this path for some way through the woods, with views of a section of the Wye not visible from the long distance route. Pass an old railway bridge on the left and shortly after this follow the path to the right of a house.

4 Go through a kissing gate onto The Warren. Soon take a right fork in the path, through the trees and keeping close to the river on the right. On leaving the wood, keep to the path across the open ground. Follow the river as this gradually curves round to the left – *on this stretch there are views across the river to the Wye Valley Walk section*. Follow a short path into woodland and head HALF LEFT up the bank and out of the wood. Turn RIGHT and follow a grassy path until near the corner of the Warren.

5 Do not cross the stile, but turn LEFT and follow the boundary of the Warren. Cross over a track by a kissing gate on the right. Keep AHEAD, on a grassy path to the left of the trees. After a while, follow the path into the trees. Follow the path AHEAD to rejoin the outward route through the kissing gate and past the house. Go up the wooden steps by the old railway bridge.

6 Turn LEFT and pass two stone benches and turn SHARP RIGHT on a tarmac path. Follow this up steps to the junction with a road – *the site of the original motte and bailey castle, built circa 1100 AD* – can be seen on the left during this section of the walk. On reaching the road, turn LEFT and LEFT again at the junction by The Swan at Hay. Follow the pavement back to the Town Clock.

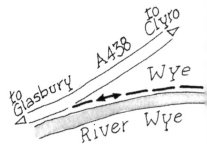

38

Hay-on-Wye

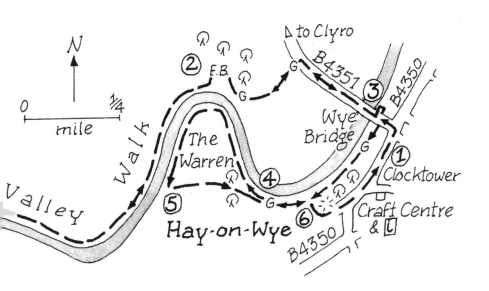

PRONUNCIATION

These basic points should help non-Welsh speakers

Welsh	English equivalent
c	always hard, as in cat
ch	as on the Scottish word loch
dd	as th in then
f	as in of
ff	as in off
g	always hard as in got
ll	no real equivalent. It is like 'th' in then, but with an 'L' sound added to it, giving 'thlan' for the pronunciation of the Welsh 'Llan'.

In Welsh the accent usually falls on the last-but-one syllable of a word.

KEY TO THE MAPS

=== Metalled road

=== Unsurfaced road or track

..... Footpath or route adjoining walk route

~~~ River or stream

⚘ Trees

G Gate

S Stile

F.B. Footbridge

⌄╹╱ Viewpoint

△ Summit

P Parking

i Tourist Information

THE COUNTRYSIDE CODE

• Be safe – plan ahead and follow any signs

• Leave gates and property as you find them

• Protect plants and animals, and take your litter home

• Keep dogs under close control

• Consider other people

The CRoW Act 2000, implemented throughout Wales in May 2005, introduced new legal rights of access for walkers to designated open country, predominantly mountain, moor, heath or down, plus all registered common land. This access can be subject to restrictions and closure for land management or safety reasons for up to 28 days a year.

Published by
Kittiwake
3 Glantwymyn Village Workshops, Glantwymyn, Machynlleth, Montgomeryshire SY20 8LY

© Text & map research: Jane Griffiths 2010
© Maps & illustrations: Kittiwake 2010
Drawings by Morag Perrott

Cover photos: *Main* – North of Llanbedr Hill.
Inset – St David's, Rhulen. David Perrott

Printed by MWL, Pontypool.

ISBN: **978 1 902302 79 9**